INDIAN
DESIGNS
FROM
ANCIENT ECUADOR

INDIAN DESIGNS
FROM
ANCIENT ECUADOR

by
Frederick W. Shaffer

DOVER PUBLICATIONS, INC.
NEW YORK

TO
My own Ecuadorean family: Lcdo. José Ricardo Carrera
Nieto; his wife, who is my daughter Susan; and their
children Catalina, Monica, Elizabet, Susanna and Federico.
My daughter Josephine, who shared Ecuador with us; and
her son Marcelo. My devoted wife Muriel, without whose
encouragement and patience this volume would never have
happened. And my mother, who first introduced me to the
beauties of the world and taught me to see them.

Published in Canada by General Publishing Company, Ltd., 30 Lesmill Road, Don Mills, Toronto, Ontario.
Published in the United Kingdom by Constable and Company, Ltd.

Indian Designs from Ancient Ecuador is a new work, first published by Dover Publications, Inc., in 1979.

DOVER *Pictorial Archive* SERIES

International Standard Book Number: 0-486-23764-8
Library of Congress Catalog Card Number: 78-65058

Manufactured in the United States of America
Dover Publications, Inc.
31 East 2nd Street
Mineola, N.Y. 11501

INTRODUCTION

This volume is neither an historical nor a scientific treatise. It is a sourcebook, a representative selection of designs taken from spindle whorls and decorative beads in the author's own collection. These intriguing objects were created by artist-craftsmen who plied their craft along Ecuador's central coast, principally in Manabí and Guayas Provinces, during the thousand-year period from 500 until 1500 A.D.

While much is now known of the peoples of ancient Ecuador and some archeological probes in that country have established the presence of civilizations there at least ten thousand years ago, studies of these early peoples and their cultures remain incomplete.*

The Objects and the Designs

Spindle whorls, or weights, and decorative beads, probably for personal adornment, are the sources of the designs on the following pages. The whorls were attached to the spindles used by spinners of yarn and thread to serve as a kind of balance wheel to sustain the spinning action required to twist plant and animal fibers into yarn and thread (see figure).

The designs were scratched, or otherwise deeply incised, into the shaped surfaces of these objects while the clay from which they were made was still damp. When decorated, the whorls and beads were placed in wood-fired

---

* Very briefly stated, the cultures of pre-Columbian Ecuador were related to the three chief geographical areas. The forest hunters of the Amazon basin in the east of the country may not have differed greatly in life patterns from the twentieth-century Jívaro. The Andean highlanders, constantly feuding among themselves, had an agrarian civilization similar to that of Peru, but less advanced. The coastal dwellers, creators of the objects illustrated here, led a relatively simple life of hunting, fishing and barter.

kilns similar to those still used today by the native potters of Ecuador.

Since little or no heat control was maintained during the firing process, the fired clay objects varied considerably in color. In the illustration captions the coloration of each piece shown has been given as either black, raw umber, burnt umber, terra-cotta or dark terra-cotta.

Once the whorls or beads were taken from the kiln and allowed to cool, color was worked into the surface designs, thus creating a two-color object. A white substance, possibly lime, and colored clays were employed in completing the decoration of these miniatures.

In the creation of the designs that cover the surfaces of the whorls and beads, the artists exercised amazing originality, made excellent use of very small spaces and displayed a great sense of design. In applying the decoration the very crudest of tools were used. The basic scraping, cutting and scribing were no doubt accomplished with such things as cactus thorns, reed stems, wood and bone scribes and gouges, and a variety of bird leg-bones of different sizes and diameters. Cut laterally, the leg-bones produced neat, small circles; cut diagonally, ovals. Crude but efficient.

The designs created by these craftsmen indicate a great appreciation of the environment and the world in which they lived. There are animals that hunters sought for food and for religious rites, and others that may represent household pets, since they appear to be wearing decorative collars.

Several species of bats are depicted, such as vampire and fruit bats. These were common to the area and were important to the people in their religious life. These mammals are shown in hanging, flying and even walking positions.

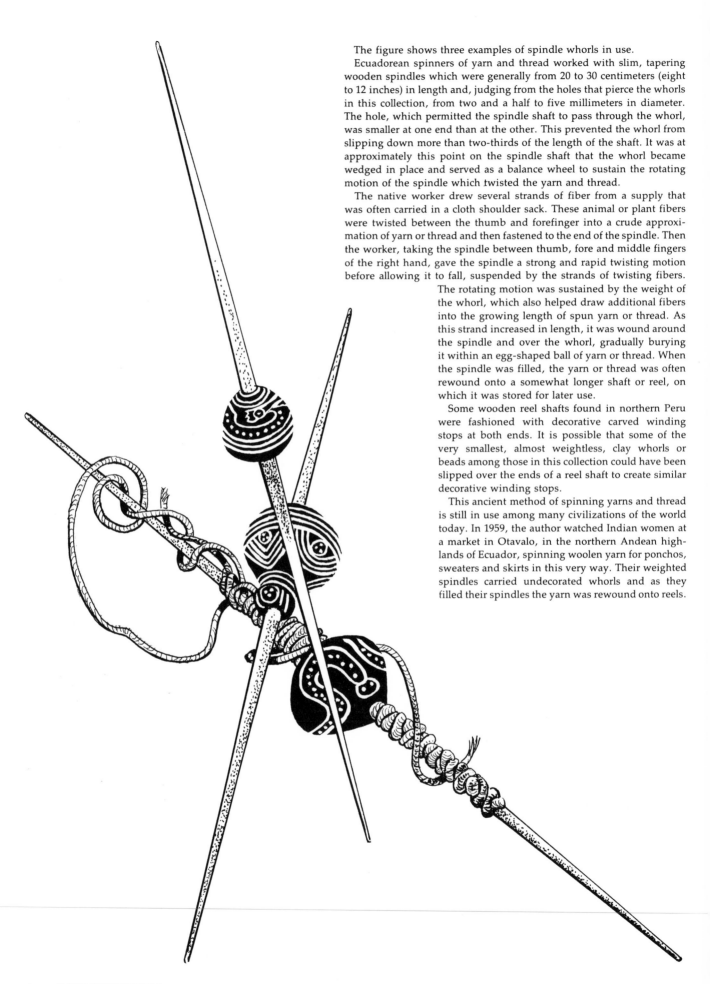

The figure shows three examples of spindle whorls in use.

Ecuadorean spinners of yarn and thread worked with slim, tapering wooden spindles which were generally from 20 to 30 centimeters (eight to 12 inches) in length and, judging from the holes that pierce the whorls in this collection, from two and a half to five millimeters in diameter. The hole, which permitted the spindle shaft to pass through the whorl, was smaller at one end than at the other. This prevented the whorl from slipping down more than two-thirds of the length of the shaft. It was at approximately this point on the spindle shaft that the whorl became wedged in place and served as a balance wheel to sustain the rotating motion of the spindle which twisted the yarn and thread.

The native worker drew several strands of fiber from a supply that was often carried in a cloth shoulder sack. These animal or plant fibers were twisted between the thumb and forefinger into a crude approximation of yarn or thread and then fastened to the end of the spindle. Then the worker, taking the spindle between thumb, fore and middle fingers of the right hand, gave the spindle a strong and rapid twisting motion before allowing it to fall, suspended by the strands of twisting fibers.

The rotating motion was sustained by the weight of the whorl, which also helped draw additional fibers into the growing length of spun yarn or thread. As this strand increased in length, it was wound around the spindle and over the whorl, gradually burying it within an egg-shaped ball of yarn or thread. When the spindle was filled, the yarn or thread was often rewound onto a somewhat longer shaft or reel, on which it was stored for later use.

Some wooden reel shafts found in northern Peru were fashioned with decorative carved winding stops at both ends. It is possible that some of the very smallest, almost weightless, clay whorls or beads among those in this collection could have been slipped over the ends of a reel shaft to create similar decorative winding stops.

This ancient method of spinning yarns and thread is still in use among many civilizations of the world today. In 1959, the author watched Indian women at a market in Otavalo, in the northern Andean highlands of Ecuador, spinning woolen yarn for ponchos, sweaters and skirts in this very way. Their weighted spindles carried undecorated whorls and as they filled their spindles the yarn was rewound onto reels.

There are many varieties of birds from both coastal and inland forest areas. Herons, pelicans, sea gulls, macaws and others are displayed. While many are readily recognizable, others seem to be symbolic representations and defy identification.

There are naturalistic representations of fish caught for food and of other sea life, such as the strange sea hare, a mollusk still to be found in warm coastal waters of North America as well as along the coasts of Central and South America.

There are conventionalized grains, grasses and what seem to be floral forms. Some of the design elements resemble seeds and parts of plants located beneath the soil.

The disembodied heads of owls, frogs and toads shown on several objects no doubt had ritualistic importance.

People wearing bird and animal masks are apparently dressed for the hunt or the ritual dance. Several seem to be in conversation and distinctions are made between their costumes.

Included are two examples of the so-called "hocker," or splayed figure, design. These strange figures resemble human beings or animals giving birth or in a coital position. Coitus is definitely represented in the second "hocker" design illustrated.

The final category is the largest. It comprises nonrepresentational designs, some of which are very complex. The term nonrepresentational is used with some reluctance. While these designs do not represent readily identifiable objects to twentieth-century observers, the original designers obviously had something specific in mind. Even in the other sections of this book, many of the identifications are admittedly conjectural because of the great gaps in our information.

Sources of the Objects and Method of Rendering

The author purchased the whorls and beads that formed the basis for his collection from street vendors of archeological artifacts in Quito, Ecuador, in 1959. Their beauty awakened his interest and he sought their source. He learned that they were then quite plentiful among the archeological diggings in Guayas and Manabí Provinces along the coast. It was from that area that this collection was to be completely assembled.

As a Foreign Service Officer with the U.S. Information Agency, the author resided in Guayaquil, Guayas Province, from 1963 until 1965. During this period many trips were made to sites in Guayas and to others in neighboring Manabí as well. Numerous excavations were made and many clay objects unearthed, including most of the whorls and beads in this collection. Curiously, at several locations, these small objects were found lying upon the sun-dried surface of the land like discarded children's marbles.

When found, the whorls and beads were generally devoid of any applied coloration. Some, however, showed signs of having once been colored. Several had white pigment deeply imbedded in the incised designs, while others carried vestiges of red and yellow pigments.

In preparing this volume, the author experimented for a time in order to determine a procedure which would allow him to record the full amount of detail in each design. It became quite apparent that if white gesso were pressed into the designs and then allowed to become nearly dry before the rounded surface was wiped clean with a damp cloth, both the intricate design and the color of the bead could be enhanced. Therefore, all of the clay whorls and beads used to illustrate this volume have had their designs refilled with white gesso. By preparing them in this way it was possible to measure and record each design with all its intricacy, faithfully and accurately. Despite the necessity to create two-dimensional illustrations of designs that originally covered spheroid or other curved shapes, great care has been taken to avoid distortions.

Accompanying each flat design there is a rendering of the shape of the original whorl or bead and the placement of each design on that shape. Then, to the extent possible, subject matter has been identified and the basic color and dimensions of each object have been indicated. This will show the skill exercised by the craftsmen who made these miniatures.

These pre-Columbian artists have left us a remarkable collection of designs that lend themselves to a multitude of applications in the ceramic, textile, metal and graphic arts. For those involved in these and other manifestations of the arts and crafts fields, the designs will provide many suggestions.

CONTENTS

ECUADOR AND NEIGHBORING
SOUTH AMERICAN COUNTRIES

Venezuela

Colombia

Ecuador

Brazil

Peru

Bolivia

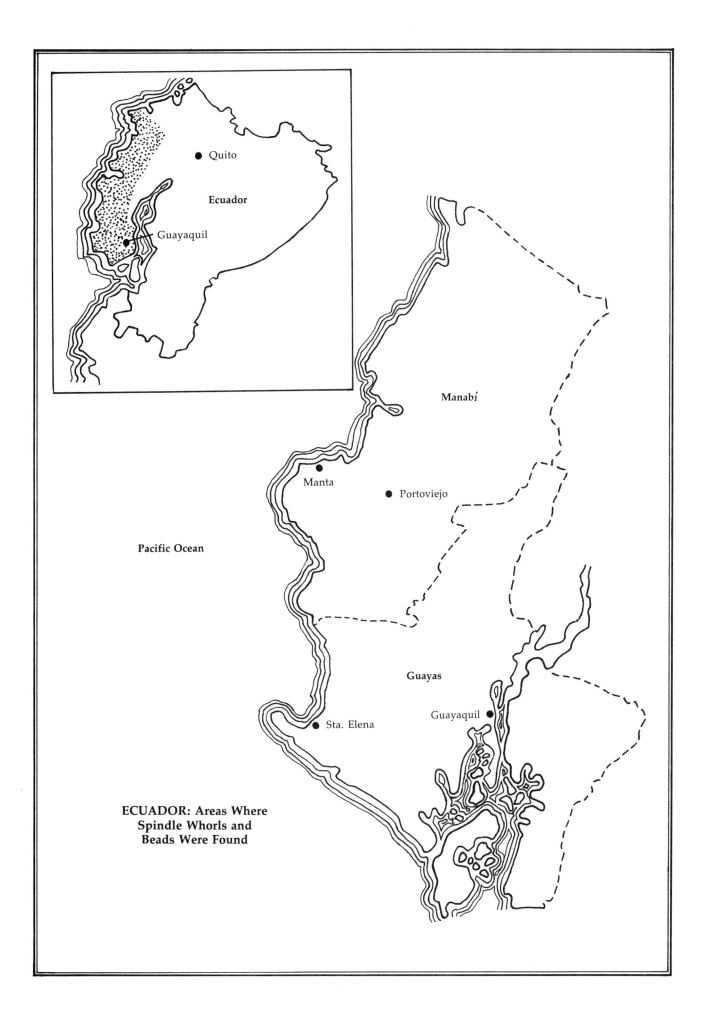

Quito

Ecuador

Guayaquil

Manabí

Manta

Portoviejo

Pacific Ocean

Guayas

Guayaquil

Sta. Elena

**ECUADOR: Areas Where
Spindle Whorls and
Beads Were Found**

INDIAN
DESIGNS
FROM
ANCIENT ECUADOR

NOTE

The captions of the first 196 illustrations contain the following information: illustration number; identification of the specific subject (sometimes conjectural); the color of the original spindle whorl or bead; and two dimensions of the original spindle whorl or bead, first its diameter at the widest point and then its height, both dimensions expressed in millimeters (25 millimeters are approximately equal to one inch).

Since illustrations 197–282 are all nonrepresentational (that is, unidentifiable), those captions contain only the illustration number, original color and original dimensions.

1
Masked dancers.
Black. 9 × 17 mm.

2
Hunters.
Black. 17 × 16 mm.

3
Masked hunters with game bags.
Terra-cotta. 12.5 × 12 mm.

4
Hunters with game bags.
Black. 10 × 11.5 mm.

5
Masked dancers.
Terra-cotta. 12 × 12 mm.

6
Masked people conversing.
Black. 11 × 13.5 mm.

7
Hocker, or splayed figure.
Black. 13.5 × 13 mm.

8
Human hocker.
Black. 15 × 13 mm.

9
Dog.
Black. 13.5 × 11 mm.

10
Crouching dog.
Burnt umber. 12 × 10 mm.

11
Dog.
Raw umber. 14 × 14 mm.

12
Seated dog.
Black. 13.5 × 12 mm.

13
Running dog.
Black. 17 × 15 mm.

14
Unidentified mammal.
Terra-cotta. 13 × 11.5 mm.

15
Unidentified mammal.
Burnt umber. 16.5 × 15 mm.

16
Dog.
Raw umber. 16 × 16.5 mm.

17
Fox.
Black. 13.5 × 11 mm.

18
Fawn.
Terra-cotta. 16 × 15 mm.

19
Fox.
Black. 14 × 10.5 mm.

20
Anteater.
Terra-cotta. 13 × 11.5 mm.

21
Unidentified mammal.
Black. 14.5 × 12 mm.

22
Kinkajou.
Black. 14 × 10 mm.

23
Mouse.
Black. 15 × 13.5 mm.

24
Opossum.
Dark terra-cotta. 13 × 11 mm.

25
Badger.
Burnt umber. 13 × 10 mm.

26
Unidentified mammal.
Burnt umber. 12 × 12 mm.

27
Dog.
Black. 15 × 14 mm.

28
Unidentified mammal.
Black. 14.5 × 12 mm.

29
Unidentified mammal.
Burnt umber. 12.5 × 10 mm.

30
Sloth.
Dark terra-cotta. 13 × 12 mm.

31
Sloth.
Black. 13.5 × 11 mm.

32
Unidentified mammal.
Black. 14 × 12 mm.

33
Unidentified mammal.
Raw umber. 17.5 × 16 mm.

34
Rabbit.
Black. 11 × 12 mm.

35
Unidentified mammal.
Black. 12.5 × 10 mm.

36
Weasel.
Terra-cotta. 14 × 14 mm.

37
Weasel.
Burnt umber. 18.5 × 14.5 mm.

38
Dog with collar.
Black. 14 × 15 mm.

39
Deer.
Burnt umber. 18 × 17 mm.

40
Monkey.
Black. 12.5 × 12 mm.

41
Spider monkey with collar.
Black. 11 × 12.5 mm.

42
Spider monkey.
Black. 13 × 15.5 mm.

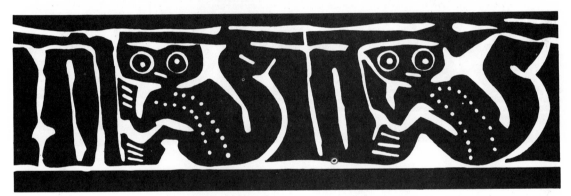

43
Monkey.
Dark terra-cotta. 13.5 × 11 mm.

44
Unidentified mammal.
Black. 12.5 × 11.5 mm.

45
Unidentified mammal.
Terra-cotta. 16 × 13.5 mm.

46
Fox.
Terra-cotta. 13 × 10 mm.

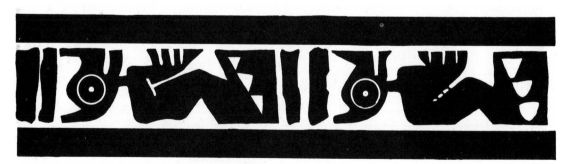

47
Squirrel.
Black. 14 × 10 mm.

48
Fawn.
Black. 12 × 13 mm.

49
Squirrel.
Black. 15.5 × 15 mm.

50
Squirrel.
Black. 14 × 12 mm.

51
Squirrel.
Black. 14.5 × 14 mm.

52
Squirrel.
Black. 15 × 13 mm.

53
Unidentified mammal.
Black. 13.5 × 12.5 mm.

54
Bat.
Black. 16.5 × 15 mm.

55
Bat.
Black. 12 × 10 mm.

56
Bat.
Black. 12.5 × 10 mm.

57
Bat.
Black. 13 × 13 mm.

58
Bat.
Terra-cotta. 11 × 12.5 mm.

59
Bat.
Black. 12 × 11 mm.

20   MAMMALS

60
Bat in flight.
Black. 12.5 × 12.5 mm.

61
Bat in hanging position.
Black. 14 × 11.5 mm.

62
Bat in walking position.
Black. 10 × 11.5 mm.

63
Bat.
Terra-cotta. 10 × 12 mm.

64
Bat.
Black. 13 × 10 mm.

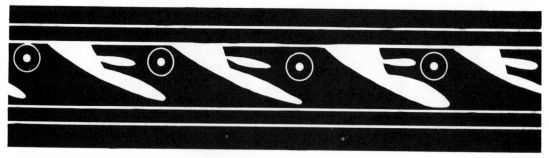

65
Sea lions.
Black. 13 × 11 mm.

66
Double-mammal form.
Black. 12 × 11.5 mm.

67
Double-mammal form.
Black. 12 × 11.5 mm.

68
Double-mammal form.
Black. 13.5 × 11 mm.

69
Water fowl.
Black. 14.5 × 12.5 mm.

70
Sea gull.
Terra-cotta. 18.5 × 15.5 mm.

71
Pelican.
Raw umber. 12.5 × 12 mm.

72
Pelican in flight.
Black. 18 × 15 mm.

73
Pelican.
Black. 18.5 × 17 mm.

74
Pelican.
Terra-cotta. 14 × 11 mm.

75
Pelican.
Black. 15.5 × 12.5 mm.

76
Pelican.
Black. 15 × 13 mm.

77
Pelican chick.
Black. 12.5 × 10.5 mm.

78
Pelican.
Black. 13 × 10 mm.

79
Pelican chick.
Black. 12 × 11.5 mm.

80
Pelican chick.
Burnt umber. 15 × 13 mm.

81
Pelican.
Black. 15.5 × 13.5 mm.

82
Pelican.
Raw umber. 13 × 13.5 mm.

83
Young pelican.
Black. 14 × 10 mm.

84
Pelican.
Black. 13.5 × 11.5 mm.

85
Sea bird.
Black. 15 × 12 mm.

86
Unidentified bird.
Black. 13 × 11.5 mm.

87
Pelican.
Black. 13 × 13 mm.

88
Pelican.
Black. 15 × 11 mm.

89
Young pelican.
Black. 14 × 14 mm.

90
Young pelican.
Terra-cotta. 16 × 15 mm.

91
Unidentified birds.
Black. 13 × 11.5 mm.

92
Heron.
Black. 13.5 × 11 mm.

93
Chick.
Black. 18 × 18.5 mm.

94
Young bird.
Black. 11.5 × 11 mm.

95
Heron.
Burnt umber. 13 × 11.5 mm.

96
Chick.
Black. 15 × 13.5 mm.

97
Young bird.
Black. 15.5 × 14 mm.

98
Young bird.
Black. 14 × 14 mm.

99
Chick.
Black. 8.5 × 11 mm.

100
Unidentified bird.
Black. 13 × 15.5 mm.

101
Unidentified bird.
Black. 13 × 10.5 mm.

102
Gull chick.
Black. 14 × 11 mm.

103
Young heron.
Dark terra-cotta. 13 × 13 mm.

104
Heron.
Black. 13 × 14 mm.

105
Unidentified bird.
Terra-cotta. 12.5 × 10 mm.

106
Unidentified bird.
Dark terra-cotta. 17 × 15 mm.

107
Unidentified bird.
Terra-cotta. 18 × 15.5 mm.

108
Heron.
Terra-cotta. 10.5 × 11 mm.

109
Heron.
Dark terra-cotta. 13.5 × 12 mm.

110
Heron.
Black. 13 × 12 mm.

111
Heron.
Black. 13 × 13 mm.

112
Heron.
Black. 12 × 13 mm.

113
Heron.
Dark terra-cotta. 13 × 15.5 mm.

114
Heron.
Terra-cotta. 11 × 15.5 mm.

115
Owl.
Dark terra-cotta. 17.5 × 17 mm.

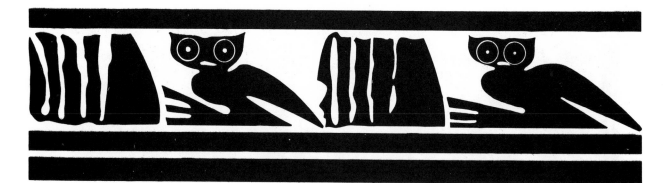

116
Owl.
Dark terra-cotta. 18 × 15 mm.

117
Owl.
Black. 12.5 × 12 mm.

118
Owl.
Black. 13 × 11 mm.

119
Owl.
Black. 12 × 11.5 mm.

120
Owl.
Black. 11.5 × 11.5 mm.

121
Owl covering prey.
Black. 12 × 10 mm.

122
Owl covering prey.
Dark terra-cotta. 17 × 15 mm.

123
Owl covering prey.
Terra-cotta. 15 × 14 mm.

124
Owl covering prey.
Terra-cotta. 18 × 15 mm.

125
Owl covering prey.
Raw umber. 18 × 15 mm.

126
Owl.
Black. 16.5 × 16.5 mm.

127
Owl.
Black. 15 × 12 mm.

128
Serpent with head detached.
Raw umber. 19 × 15 mm.

129
Serpent.
Black. 25 × 17 mm.

130
Serpent.
Black. 24 × 18 mm.

131
Serpent with head detached.
Raw umber. 18 × 15 mm.

132
Serpent with head detached.
Raw umber. 19 × 17 mm.

133
Conventionalized serpent form.
Raw umber. 21 × 15 mm.

134
Serpent with head detached.
Black. 22 × 15 mm.

135
Serpent beneath the soil.
Black. 19 × 20 mm.

136
Serpent form.
Terra-cotta. 16 × 16 mm.

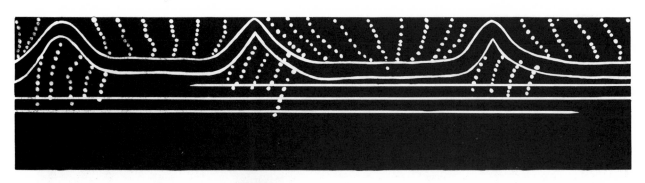

137
Serpent passing through the earth.
Burnt umber. 18 × 14 mm.

138
Serpent with head detached.
Raw umber. 19 × 17 mm.

139
Caiman or crocodile.
Burnt umber. 20 × 18 mm.

140
Crocodile.
Black. 17 × 15.5 mm.

141
Young crocodile.
Black. 13 × 11.5 mm.

142
Caiman or crocodile.
Burnt umber. 12.5 × 10 mm.

143
Crocodile.
Black. 10 × 12 mm.

144
Iguana.
Black. 14 × 12.5 mm.

145
Iguana.
Black. 16 × 12 mm.

146
Lizard.
Black. 13 × 11.5 mm.

147
Lizard.
Black. 12 × 12 mm.

148
Lizard.
Black. 14.5 × 11.5 mm.

149
Lizard.
Black. 13.5 × 12 mm.

150
Lizard.
Black. 13 × 10 mm.

151
Lizard/iguana, skeletal form.
Black. 15.5 × 12.5 mm.

152
Lizard/iguana, skeletal form.
Black. 14.5 × 13.5 mm.

153
Lizard/iguana, skeletal form.
Black. 15.5 × 12.5 mm.

154
Slug.
Black. 14 × 12 mm.

155
Slug.
Black. 13 × 11.5 mm.

156
Slug or mollusk.
Black. 13 × 12 mm.

157
Lizard, adult and young.
Black. 12.5 × 9.5 mm.

158
Fish.
Dark terra-cotta. 16 × 13.5 mm.

159
Fish, skeletal form.
Black. 13.5 × 15.5 mm.

160
Fish, skeletal form.
Raw umber. 15.5 × 12 mm.

161
Fish, skeletal form.
Dark terra-cotta. 13 × 12 mm.

162
Flounder or halibut.
Black. 13 × 11 mm.

163
Fish form.
Black. 13 × 13 mm.

164
Fish or dolphin.
Terra-cotta. 12 × 10 mm.

165
Fish or dolphin.
Black. 12 × 10 mm.

166
Sea-creature form.
Black. 15 × 14 mm.

167
Seated frog.
Black. 11.5 × 12 mm.

168
Crayfish.
Black. 14.5 × 13 mm.

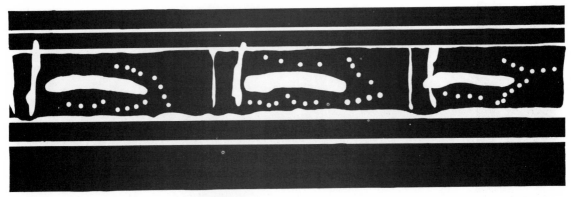

169
Unidentified aquatic creature.
Black. 18 × 17 mm.

170
Sea hare.
Raw umber. 15 × 14 mm.

171
Unidentified aquatic creature.
Black. 14 × 13 mm.

172
Small fish.
Raw umber. 12 × 10 mm.

173
Small fish.
Raw umber. 12 × 10 mm.

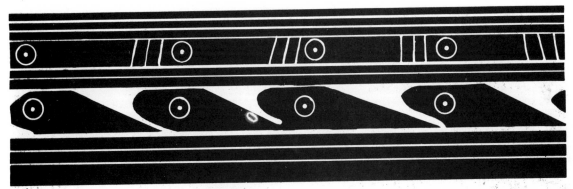

174
Dolphin or porpoise.
Black. 12 × 10.5 mm.

175
Dolphin or porpoise.
Black. 10 × 10 mm.

176
Grain.
Raw umber. 18 × 13.5 mm.

177
Grain.
Black. 20 × 16.5 mm.

178
Seeds and grain.
Raw umber. 15 × 13.5 mm.

179
Grain.
Raw umber. 14 × 13.5 mm.

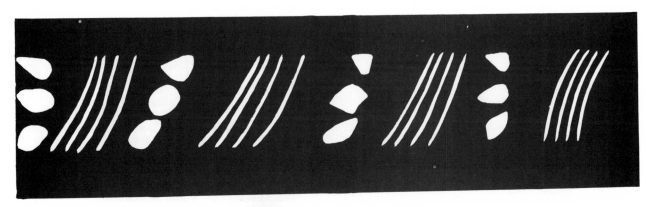

180
Grain.
Raw umber. 16 × 13.5 mm.

181
Grain.
Black. 15 × 13 mm.

182
Grain.
Black. 16 × 14 mm.

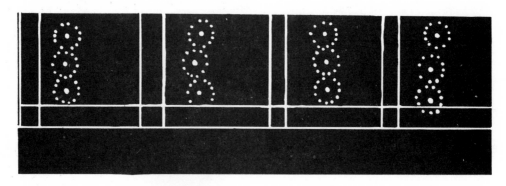

183
Flower form.
Dark terra-cotta. 11.5 × 11.5 mm.

184
Flower form.
Terra-cotta. 12.5 × 10 mm.

185
Flower form.
Dark terra-cotta. 14 × 10 mm.

186
Flower form.
Black. 15 × 14 mm.

187
Plant and sun.
Black. 15 × 12.5 mm.

188
Frog head.
Dark terra-cotta. 16 × 13 mm.

189
Owl head.
Black. 13 × 12 mm.

190
Frog head.
Burnt umber. 14 × 12.5 mm.

191
Frog head.
Black. 14 × 12 mm.

192
Frog head.
Black. 15 × 13 mm.

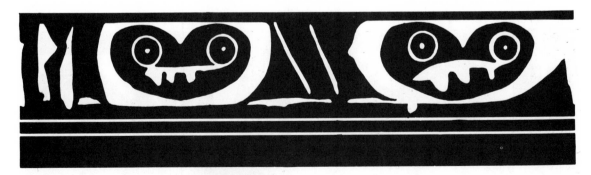

193
Frog head.
Black. 16 × 13 mm.

194
Frog head.
Raw umber. 16.5 × 15 mm.

195
Frog head.
Black. 16 × 12.5 mm.

196
Frog head.
Black. 14 × 11 mm.

197
Raw umber. 11 × 14 mm.

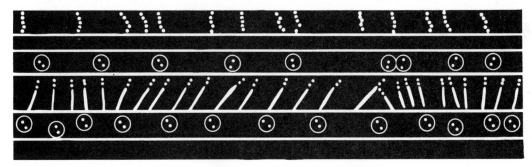

198
Raw umber. 19.5 × 18 mm.

199
Burnt umber. 17 × 16 mm.

200
Raw umber. 21 × 21 mm.

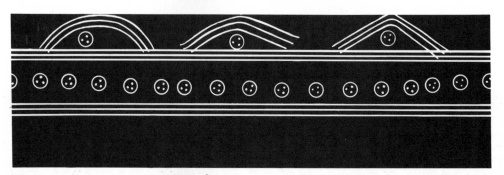

201
Raw umber. 18 × 16.5 mm.

202
Black. 20 × 22 mm.

203
Raw umber. 21 × 20.

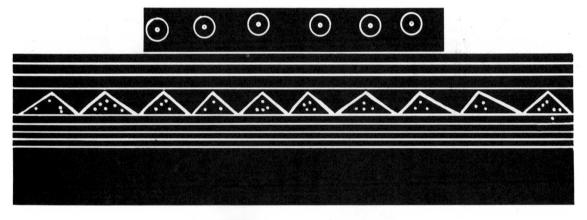

204
Raw umber. 21 × 22 mm.

205
Raw umber. 20.5 × 16 mm.

NONREPRESENTATIONAL   69

206
Black. 16 × 15 mm.

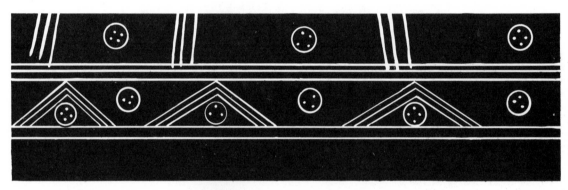

207
Black. 18.5 × 15 mm.

208
Raw umber. 22.5 × 20 mm.

209
Black. 15.5 × 13 mm.

210
Black. 19 × 17.5 mm.

211
Black. 16.5 × 15 mm.

212
Raw umber. 18 × 16.5 mm.

213
Terra-cotta. 16 × 14.5 mm.

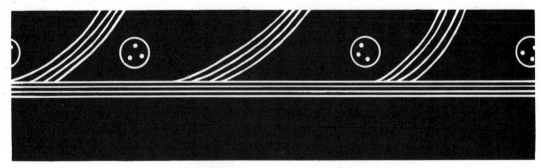

214
Raw umber. 20 × 16.5 mm.

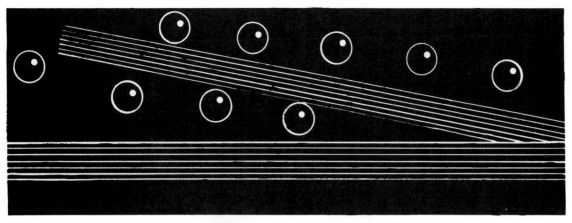

215
Black. 17 × 16.5 mm.

216
Terra-cotta. 19 × 17 mm.

217
Raw umber. 24 × 20 mm.

218
Black. 16 × 15 mm.

219
Black. 15.5 × 14 mm.

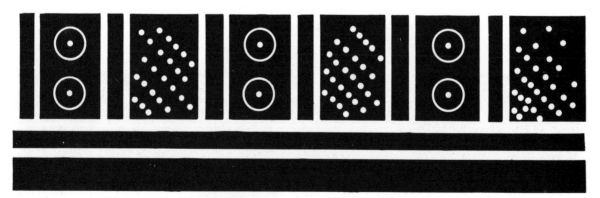

220
Black. 16 × 14.5 mm.

221
Black. 17 × 18 mm.

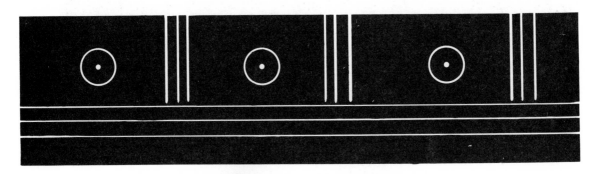

222
Black. 16 × 14 mm.

223
Terra-cotta. 15 × 12 mm.

224
Black. 15 × 14 mm.

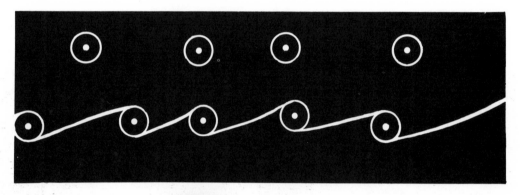

225
Black. 12 × 13 mm.

226
Black. 18 × 16 mm.

227
Terra-cotta. 10 × 10 mm.

228
Black. 17 × 17 mm.

229
Terra-cotta. 13 × 11.5 mm.

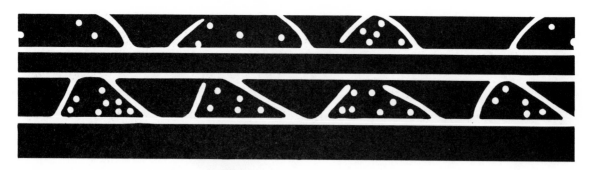

230
Burnt umber. 21 × 16 mm.

231
Raw umber. 18.5 × 16 mm.

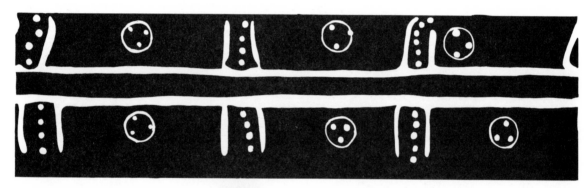

232
Raw umber. 21.5 × 18 mm.

233
Raw umber. 20 × 12 mm.

234
Black. 21 × 15 mm.

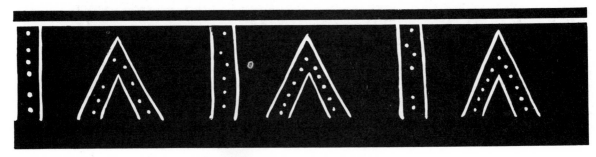

235
Black. 24 × 17 mm.

236
Black. 13 × 15 mm.

237
Raw umber. 16.5 × 17 mm.

238
Black. 13 × 13 mm.

239
Black. 19 × 18 mm.

240
Black. 13.5 × 11.5 mm.

241
Black. 13.5 × 10 mm.

242
Black. 15 × 13.5 mm.

243
Black. 15.5 × 16 mm.

244
Raw umber. 15 × 13 mm.

245
Raw umber. 17 × 17.5 mm.

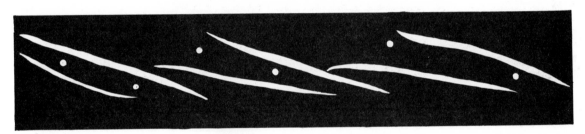

246
Raw umber. 18 × 11 mm.

247
Raw umber. 17.5 × 14 mm.

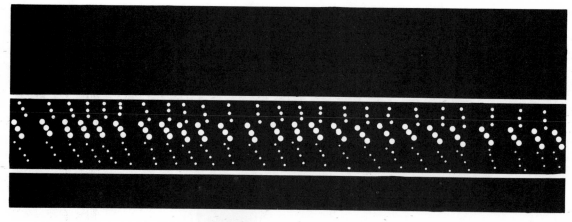

248
Terra-cotta. 16 × 17.5 mm.

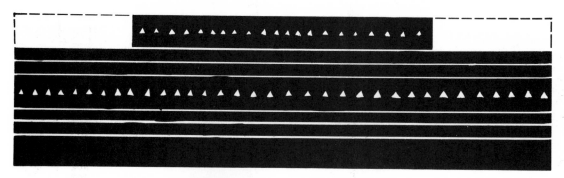

249
Raw umber. 16 × 14.5 mm.

250
Raw umber. 18 × 13.5 mm.

251
Raw umber. 22 × 12 mm.

252
Raw umber. 25 × 17 mm.

253
Raw umber. 22.5 × 12.5 mm.

254
Black. 22 × 18 mm.

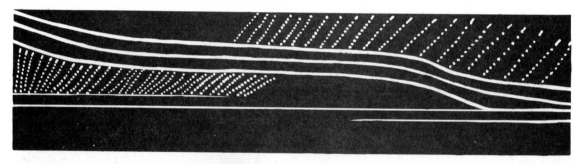

255
Raw umber. 23 × 17 mm.

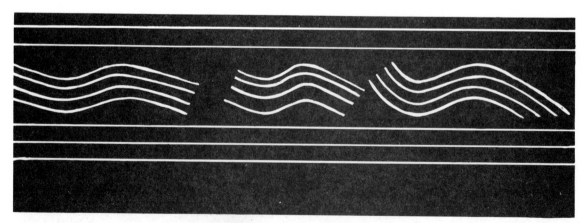

256
Raw umber. 19 × 20 mm.

257
Raw umber. 22 × 17 mm.

258
Raw umber. 17.5 × 14 mm.

259
Black. 15.5 × 14 mm.

260
Raw umber. 13 × 10 mm.

261
Terra-cotta. 14 × 12 mm.

262
Black. 15 × 14 mm.

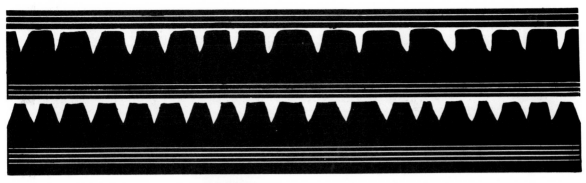

263
Black. 13 × 11 mm.

264
Black. 13 × 11 mm.

265
Terra-cotta. 13 × 10 mm.

266
Black. 16.5 × 15.5 mm.

267
Black. 18.5 × 16 mm.

268
Black. 15.5 × 15 mm.

269
Terra-cotta. 24 × 14 mm.

270
Black. 13 × 11.5 mm.

271
Black. 14.5 × 12.5 mm.

272
Burnt umber. 14 × 13.5 mm.

273
Black. 13 × 10 mm.

274
Raw umber. 16 × 14 mm.

275
Black. 14.5 × 13 mm.

276
Black. 18 × 16.5 mm.

277
Black. 13 × 12 mm.

278
Black. 16 × 11.5 mm.

279
Black. 14 × 13.5 mm.

280
Terra-cotta. 14 × 11 mm.

281
Black. 12 × 11.5 mm.

282
Black. 15.5 × 15 mm.